AUGUSTINE'S VISION

Also by Peter Filkins

What She Knew

After Homer

AUGUSTINE'S VISION

poems by

PETER FILKINS

new american press

milwaukee, wis.

new american press

Printed in the United States of America

ISBN 978-0-9817802-9-0

For ordering information, please contact:

Ingram Book Group
One Ingram Blvd.
La Vergne, TN 37086
(800) 937-8000
orders@ingrambook.com

ACKNOWLEDGMENTS

My thanks goes out to the following periodicals in which the poems listed have appeared or are forthcoming, some of them in slightly different form:

The Iowa Review	"Owen's Shark"
	"Rocky"
Narrative	"The Wild Boar"
Sewanee Review	"The Broken Piano"
	"The Sea"
The American Scholar	"Water Lilies"
Southwest Review	"Vermeer"
American Arts Quarterly	"Constable's Clouds"
Salamander	"Beanbag Toss"
Fulcrum Annual	"Augustine's Vision"

The following poems also appear on the website lyrikline.org in English and in German translation: "Augustine's Vision," "Dismantling the Birches," "The Hunters," and "The Wild Boar." "Vermeer" received the 2007 Elizabeth Matchett Stover Memorial Award from *Southwest Review,* and "The Wild Boar" was named a Finalist by *Narrative* in its 2009 Poetry Contest.

I also wish to thank The MacDowell Colony for residencies that provided valuable time to generate many of these poems, and the American Academy in Berlin for a Berlin Prize Fellowship. Thanks also to Bard College at Simon's Rock for a sabbatical leave. Very special thanks to Rosanna Warren and Lawrence Raab, who read the manuscript at a crucial juncture and provided numerous useful suggestions.

To Peter H. Begley
in friendship

CONTENTS

There is a time when feeling knows two things:
The dead bird lying, and the whir of wings.

Howard Moss

AUGUSTINE'S VISION

AUGUSTINE'S VISION

Many years later, while contemplating beauty
as order, he would think of them: gamecocks
sharpening their claws for a scrap, and how
in the market's dusty tumult he felt compelled
to stop and watch them while on his way
to be baptized and confess himself a creature of sin.

Prisoner to his heart's regard, he courted error,
the beauty of a thing in and of itself
not always the same as God's invisible plan,
the gamecocks and their darting, skillful parries,
the exultant crowing, bodies taut with power,
soon edging the crowd towards a rippling frenzy.

"For what horizon do eyes of love not scan,
hoping for a hint of reason's beautiful scheme,"
he later wrote, thinking of savage birds
pitched in battle, pure animal action
without mind – limp wings and carriage, a croak
gone awry, all of it fitting nature's set way.

Though this was years before he lay on his deathbed,
Hippo surrounded, the Vandal hordes approaching,
himself lamenting his sins, remembering gamecocks,
their beaks and talons bloodied, no doubt convinced
a higher mind worked through them, ordering all things,
as the saint continued weeping inside his narrow cell.

VERMEER

The Art of Painting, ca. 1666

I

The news from Delft is still the same:
plague has returned, the ships have left,
while further north the sea at Haarlem
is flat and gray, clear as the deft
chill lens that amplifies this room
unto itself, history being elsewhere
and unknowable. Though Clio may consume
provinces, countries, her golden hair
is wrapped in laurel, securely intact,
while what remains is what is seen
in deep perspective, the painted fact
of light that dwells, this dwelling scene.

II

Another child is dead and buried,
the clay clods raining upon his casket
no longer heard, lost to the harried
wastes of time where an angel's trumpet
lifts its muted anthem towards infinity.
Still the music plays, each note
expressed through an anonymity
treasured by lovers, lining the rote
familiar charm of each everyday task
stretched on a canvas's snowy expanse,
as the moment congeals, alive in a mask
whose life is an art attuned to silence.

III

The map of things is enigmatic:
a room, a girl, a trumpet's sheen.
Yet what peels back the curtain's fabric
enlivens what the mind has seen.
Her limp blonde curls, demure blue dress
pooling color like a low-lit flame,
are but the holy surfaces
of life embroidered by a frame.
Beyond this, nothing. Rumors, death,
the sky a leaden plate above.
By canvas skin, by brush's breath,
master, you no doubt were loved.

ROCKY

As the fastball released, spinning and spinning
to slide invincibly low and away, how could
I know (the umpire calling me out, out
went the roar of the crowd into the grassy air)
that years later, blear-eyed mad, he'd place

the gun in his mouth, maybe think twice
about the mess he'd leave behind, certainty
however triumphing over the future
blank empty of her touch, her smile
no more now than heartsick scorching flame

triggering the radical inner explosion
of a life gone to pieces, Rocky! Rocky!
his father bellowed from the backdoor steps
as we played on and on in the sandlot,
practicing the useless beautiful skills

of our Little League, pop fly and grounder,
toss and catch, there in the low red glare
of a late inning's summer sunset that,
come Saturday, would freeze my stance,
blind me to the pitch, I never saw it coming.

GIRL, 2, PULLED FROM POND

Was it the light
    that caught you,
recondite
    as angel breath,
was it the light
    that drew you
in your summer dress?

Was it the song
    of a blackbird
con–quer–ing'
    with its call,
was it the song
    of a blackbird,
and that was all?

Was it the scent
    of sweet clover
that, dizzying, sent
    you into the field,
was it the scent
    of sweet clover,
that so appealed?

Was it the cool
    feel of water,
the pond's muddy ooze
    sucking each toe,
was it the cool
    feel of water
that tempted you so?

A jitterbug shadow
    with wide-open arms
crossing the meadow
    that parted like air;
soon everywhere howls
    sown by alarm
and you not there.

BEANBAG TOSS

for my sister

About the size of a book.
Homemade. Filled with
a pound of navy beans
sewn into corduroy swatches
of your worn-out, crimson
best-for-playground jeans.

All morning we'd watch
cartoons while tossing
its nubbed, gravelly weight
between us on the rug,
dust kicking up in motes
aswirl with each new chuck

across the cellar playroom,
the comfort of its heft
exiting my hand to sail,
in memory, the length
of air emptied as
you caught it, then left.

THE BROKEN PIANO

Have all your melodies left you,
    your keyboard idle as dentures,
voided now of its raggedy tunes?

Even so, time still plays you,
    abandoned in this drafty barn,
where at night the mouse's struggle

ekes out its panicked syncopation
    beneath the owl's wheeling shadow
as a shutter clatters in the manic wind.

Winter having chilled you, summer
    expanding your sound board's grain,
music, like desolation, has become

for you an opus cordoned off
    by shrieks and groans, broken strings
whose memory of a hammer's blow

is sweetened by a finger's touch
    somewhere coaxing out a last scherzo
before dissonant, cold neglect set in.

And yet you remain, upright, serene,
    your impassive bulk anchoring the dark
hushed rafters, the hayloft poised to hear

the concert of your ruin, silence
    the answering choir whose crescendo
is final and certain, harrowing the applause.

DISMANTLING THE BIRCHES

for James Lasdun

"Topped, dropped & chipped 2 dead white birch trees"
reads the bill arriving one week later.
The damage? "Labor & Equipment – $250,"
though it's no sure bargain: blithe empty air
now all that's left of what once stood, who knows,
a lifetime? a century?, their tall, swaying might
reduced to firewood we'll burn this winter.

Still, it was time. The birches too near the house,
ten days ago a heavy limb broke loose,
waking us with a *thunk* so loud we thought
the end of sleep had come, our roof done in
and leaking through November's bony cold
until next morning workers broke the news:
nothing for it, those trees were coming down.

Summer. Morning. A locust's reedy whine,
the day a promise caught in each flickering leaf,
as a boy I loved their white thrusting shoots
rising like a massive V outside my window,
each trunk's diameter twice my arm across,
the scarred papery bark a sheet inscribed
with twists and leanings, weather written in.

How many summers had they seen? How many kites
had disemboweled flight among their branches?
And who could know what kind of pure good luck
had let them grow so tall, lightning blasts
and hail, drought and shearing winds, the gamut
of experience as like to strike them down
as nurture lasting reach into a pale blue sky.

I blink my eyes, but yes, they're really gone,
leaving behind an absence that becomes them,
sawdust and firewood cleared away as well,
the view pried open to reveal a landscape,
one never really seen before – that hilltop,
iron gray in autumn, a stillness loud with geese
on their necessary flight above the trees.

THE HUNTERS

for Susan

Dawn's pewter quiet
erupts with a blast
of shotguns on the lake,
jolting us awake
from our halting sleep.

The hunters are back,
predictable as fall's
scarlet plash
of calendar maples.
Camouflaged, funereal

in their whispered
death-bed watch
behind a makeshift blind,
their fitful *quack-ack-acks*
imitate the call

of a wounded duck
that in fact sounds drunk,
each belching shot
an attempt at validation
in the face of failure.

Sweetheart, the blaze
of morning is upon us
here in our downy bed.
Come closer. Let's kiss.
Whatever's insinuated

by the chuck of water,
far fields of fresh cut hay,
may it be this
slow animation
of lips and arms and breasts

under the snug duvet
you lift like a vaulted wing,
our bodies warm as
rose light firing the hills
of this furious season.

THE SEA

Eugène Boudin, 1824-1898

Next to it, the mind lets go,
   grasping at particulars:
a buoy riding the leaden swell,
   sea gulls tacking the wind,
or farther off, almost immobile
   against the horizon's haze
of salt humidity, a schooner
   plying through waves,
the sleekness of its wooden hull
   knifing towards home.

And so, lost in continuities,
   our need of them: harbors
dotted with rocks, jetties anchoring
   the ships, and beaches strewn
with vacationers whose casual thoughts
   while strolling on sand might be
about the news from home, trouble
   in the markets, or the meaning
of shifts in the afternoon's weather
   infusing this coastal scene

which you have given us, Monsieur Boudin,
   Deauville. La plage, marée basse
possessing still what simply was
   for you "a lively tenderness
for those eternal things which so many
   unhappy beings pass,
and will always pass, without seeing,"
   the schooner closing fast
on harbor and jetty, sandbar and beach,
   the tidal low of the amorphous sea.

CONSTABLE'S CLOUDS

for Fred H. Stocking

I

Scudding through distances, hovering in blue
vacuities of a summer's day, cumuli
float upon the surface of a ranging eye
that studies their shape, analyzes their hue

in pigments now aswirl upon the palette,
soft collisions of white and spectral grey
soon weathering the canvas, capturing a day
whose transience we know because he saw it

there in the changeable sky he stood beneath,
stratus and nimbus, thunderhead and puff
fixed in their currency, the consequence of
the raw prevailing wind on Hampstead Heath.

II

"No two days are alike, nor even two hours,"
and so his brush keeps on the move while he
does not, despising those who continually
ignore their craft by "running after pictures."

Weymouth, Harrow, Flatford, Dedham Vale,
ephemera beneath the sky's broad radius
casting England's neutral air on all that is
and eludes him, be it fame, or more so the pale

"evening light off a dark grey effect – looking
eastwards" toward a drifting bank of cloud
that's there, then gone, someone in the crowd
later calling his picture "a nasty green thing."

III

Maria coughs again, the taste of blood
causing a cloud of fear to pass across
her feverish bright-eyed gaze. Soon loss
will fell him. "Every gleam of sunshine blighted,

can it be wondered I paint continual storms?"
Each gathering front, each rising eastern gale
turbid now with grief, as wind and hail
consume a placid landscape, unleashing forms

that build and threaten, yet do not release
him from the sadness planted in his heart,
the demands of composition, the rigor of art
as equal to rain as sun, adversity as peace.

IV

"I shall never feel again as I have felt,
the face of the world is totally changed to me."
And yet the sketches continue, originality
hard won upon the back of a life that's dealt

with setback by studying atmospheric effects.
"Clouds. Moving very fast. With occasional
very bright openings to the blue," the residual
of an altocumulus inhabiting the flex

of a brushstroke, "wind after rain in morning"
the note he jots to catalogue the weather
he'll use, if not survive, observing much later,
"in truth, my art is another word for feeling."

SOLITAIRE

When I saw *The Downfall* in Berlin,
the theater just around the corner
from the long-buried bunker, I couldn't believe
Frau Goebbels would sit down to a game
of solitaire after having just killed
all six of her children as they slept,
cyanide preferable to what she imagined
the Russians would do once they moved in.

Who, after all, could maintain such composure?
Especially at such a time, lamps flickering
out and then on like the Führer's rages,
her children having expired with a shudder
echoed on screen by the bunker's quaking.

I couldn't accept it. Too ironic
a turn, too convenient a portrayal,
the director telling us this is what started it,
millions of dead and wounded the result
of repression, the will to power, a woman
snapping down cards to the rattle of gunfire.

But what if it was like that, Frau Goebbels
unable to think of anything better to do
amid such ruin, except to wait
for her beloved Reich to finally topple
and release her from her nightmare?

The next day, visiting Sachsenhausen,
I learned about a group of prisoners
who at night had continued practicing
scales and arpeggios, a Dvořák quartet,
secretly in the hold of the pathology lab
where by day the bodies were dissected
in search of abnormalities, myself
transfixed while I sat there listening
to the audio guide, the prisoners' seeming
need for dignity in the teeth of death
comprised of a courage few of us know.

Or could hope to, trapped as we are
by certain limitations, no one surviving
who witnesses the woman playing solitaire,
the man inside the refurbished museum
thinking about a handful of musicians
practicing a transcription of Schubert's Eighth,
elusive and abandoned, unfinished forever.

THE WILD BOAR

Was it Kiki or Heinz who we hitched
that ride with from Hamburg to Berlin
twenty years ago, the sun setting across
the barren expanse of a North Sea marsh
as the car (an out-of-service ambulance)
pulled onto the transit highway from which
no exit was allowed except to stop,

wait for the East German cops to show up
and question the driver and his passengers
as to why we'd halted the car and delayed
our scheduled arrival in Berlin, surrounded
as we were by borderless frozen fields
vacant as the eyes of that policeman
unable, or at least unwilling to believe

we'd hit something in the dark which – bang! –
was there and gone, the driver turning
onto the gravel shoulder as we got out
to assess the damage done, the headlight
shattered and caved in, while at the edge,
caught in the twisted chrome and there
for the cop to inspect, the bristles of a boar

we'd hit which none of us could see
or saw as it crossed into our path
all those years ago, the wind slicing
through us, that transit highway bleak
as the thought of tomorrow among
the closed-off reaches where that boar still ran,
wounded and mortal – was it Gabi? was it Fritz?

CHINATOWN

That night over dinner when he told me
about the affair that he'd been having
as his wife lay dying, her lungs awash
with cancer, his voice betraying a wave
of guilt that would soon pull him under,

I thought of *Chinatown*, and how
Jack Nicholson can't see the future
as the past coming at him, Faye Dunaway
being no more than the ravishing
vehicle of his own familiar doom.

The evil we do can seem so accidental,
our best intentions somehow misleading us,
and yet John Huston's craggy gentility
is there to remind us how very petty
and self-serving great wrongs often are.

Which explains nothing, of course, nor would
we want it to, just as in the voice
of my friend I heard those ravages
let loose like so much displaced water
scouring down the gorges outside of L.A.,

while in the end Jack Nicholson remains
stunned on a street corner, wanting
only to keep a woman from being hurt,
yet insuring she was, the sympathy we feel
too easily embraced to be understood.

OWEN'S SHARK

I

When young Harold caught it, reeling it in,
raucous, incredulous laughter soon ceasing
as his father helped him land the shark,
then beat its head in, hammering, hammering
until the great gray length of it lay still,

no one could imagine that later, unable
to resist another peek at triumph
before bedtime, he'd find the shark
standing upright on its tail, alive
and menacing as he ran to Wilfred,

begging him come see it, which soon
he did, the boys later convincing their father
to let the fish go, take it back to the bay
where for weeks they saw it swimming
in the cold swift waters of the Irish Sea.

II

"It is a great life," Wilfred later wrote,
oblivious to "the ghostly glimmering of guns,
the hollow crashing of the shells," the front
feeling like "neither France nor England,
but a kind of paddock where the beasts
are kept a few days before the shambles,"

as he was, dying a week before war's end,
leading his platoon across a muddy canal
they'd captured, then lost, then captured again
without him, who had reminded his mother,
"There is no danger, or if any, it will be
well over before you read these lines."

III

And so the shark swam, portside
to the *Astraea*, Greek goddess of justice,
launched on the day of Wilfred's birth,
but cruising now off the coast of Africa,
the armistice signed, while Harold was sure

the man who sat in his cabin before him
was indeed Wilfred, silent and smiling,
his eyes "alive with the familiar look
of trying to make me understand,"
though what it was he didn't know

in the warm waters north of Alexandria,
where legend has it that a shark
escorting any ship is thought a sign
of a good day's catch, harbor nets teeming
with the pale, bruised bodies of the dead.

WATER LILIES

Claude Monet, 1917

Meanwhile he painted them – lilies
floating on the surface of a pond
he'd constructed "for the pleasure of the eye
and motifs to paint" at century's end,
the new one begun with multiple explosions
of carmine, coral, white fleshy flowers
against the backdrop of a subsurface blue

with distances, the sky itself reflected
in the watery sway where a cloud adrift
would later be captured by his brush
in motion, each day in the studio
another one spent to the echo of guns
bombarding the trenches, pummeling the Somme
erupting in billows of char-black smoke

upon a horizon no longer present
but subsumed, erased, immersed as he was
in the fusion of oil and water, flowers
afloat on the air beneath a willow
and its weeping, our only perspective
in a lost world lost to bottomless translucency,
the eye that sees it, and the intractable sun.

NOTES

Augustine's Vision – The quote is from Augustine's *Order in the Universe* as cited by Garry Wills in his biography of *Saint Augustine* (Viking 1999).

The Sea – The lines quoted are from a letter of Boudin's cited in Ruth L. Benjamin's monograph, *Eugène Boudin* (Raymond & Raymond 1937).

Constable's Clouds – After his marriage to Maria Bicknell in 1816, John Constable spent several summers making a series of quick oil studies of clouds in the sky over Suffolk, on the back of which he would often record the date, time of day, and the weather conditions. Intended as sketches to help him with the clouds and skies of his larger works, these are now viewed as important influences on the work of Delacroix and the Impressionists. The quotes cited in the poem are either from Constable's own comments on the back of the sketches or from his lectures on painting.

Owen's Shark – Details and quotes in the poem are from Jon Stallworthy's biography of *Wilfred Owen* (Oxford 1974).

Water Lilies – The quote is from Monet's 1893 letter to the municipal authorities of Giverny asking for permission to divert water from the river Epte in order to create a pond for aquatic plants. It is cited in Michel Hoog's *The Nymphéas of Claude Monet at the Musée de l'Orangerie* (Réunion des Musées Nationaux 1990).

PETER FILKINS is the author of two previous books of poems, *What She Knew* (1998) and *After Homer* (2002). The recipient of a Berlin Prize Fellowship in 2005 from The American Academy in Berlin, he is also the translator of Ingeborg Bachmann's collected poems, *Darkness Spoken* (2006), her novels *The Book of Franza* and *Requiem for Fanny Goldmann* (1999), and H.G. Adler's novels *The Journey* (2008) and *Panorama* (2011). He has been awarded the Stover Prize in Poetry from *Southwest Review*, as well as fellowships from the Massachusetts Cultural Council, Yaddo, MacDowell, and the Millay Colony for the Arts. His work has appeared in numerous publications, including *The New York Times Book Review*, *Poetry*, *Partisan Review*, *The New Republic*, *The American Scholar*, and the *Los Angeles Times Book Review*. He teaches writing and literature at Bard College at Simon's Rock in Great Barrington, Massachusetts.